THE SILENT MOCCASINS

MOCCASINS

TOOTIMAH

By

John G. Makie

ISBN: 1-4140-5373-8 (e-book)
ISBN: 1-4140-5372-X (Paperback)

This book is printed on acid free paper.

1stBooks - rev. 02/04/04

Introduction

I was born in a hamlet in Northern Ontario, in Canada. My father was born in Finland. He came to Canada as an immigrant and then became a Canadian citizen. In his travels he met an Indian fellow named Jim Chief and his wife Tootimah. They taught my father about living off the land in the bush of Northern Ontario.

My father also worked as a sawyer in a sawmill and operated a machine that carried logs to be cut into lumber or railroad ties. He also would stake out timber claims for paper mill companies.

When I was a boy I went with my dad on many of his trapping trips as well as when he staked out timber claims. And it was during those times that I, too, had the good fortune to meet Jim Chief and his wife Tootimah. I saw Jim as a possible ancestor of the Inca Indians of South America, and while I don't know if it was true, it gave Jim a certain kind of mystique in my young mind. I imagined he had the ability to levitate while walking on dry leaves. And that he could carry heavy objects with no effort over long distances. The Indian custom was not to have a formal burial upon death. And the Indians had no known records of birth or death.

Chapter One

We lived in an old abandoned sawmill settlement that only had six families. We could take a village census before breakfast. The folks in the settlement were all individual in their own way. And they took care not to bother each other. That made it comfortable for everyone. After all we had to survive very cold winters, and there were no service stores close by. It was twenty-two miles by railroad and seventeen miles by boat or canoe to the nearest village and in wintertime we used skis. The train ran twice a week, you would send your orders in on Friday and you would get them back on Monday. My mother liked it.

We were all of different ethnic backgrounds, English, French, Finnish, Swedish and Ukrainian. There wasn't much point in socializing because we could hardly understand each other anyway. We all lived close by the railroad track so when a train went by, you sure knew it, the house shook. But we got used to that.

There is one early July day that I especially remember. That's because my brother was home from the school that he attended in town twenty-two miles west. It was early in the morning. And Mrs. Poquette, our neighbor who lived about a half a block away, had a large pile of woven floor mats on her porch. So we asked our mother what she thought Mrs. Poquette was up to. She said, She will lay the floor mats out and make a path to the railroad track because she is expecting her husband on the local train that comes through on Friday morning.

We asked mother how often has she done this because her husband has been dead for some time now. Oh! yes she said but she thinks it will happen that he is coming home. We do not bother with her because it is her buisness.

The space between each of us was so that during the heavy winter snows we were unable to reach each other's place except with snowshoes or skis. We sure learned how to live alone.

Little Joe Dagg was only five foot four and his common law wife was only known as Mrs. Heath. She was five foot seven and weighed about two hundred and forty pounds. Joe would get quite yappy when he got drunk on their dandelion wine, which was very potent. One sunny afternoon in the winter we were playing outside and saw Joe come flying out his back door and land in the snow bank. Joe was kicking and screaming all the way into the snow. Good entertainment. Mrs. Heath was a very kind and generous lady except, sometime, with Joe.

Then there was old Victor the Finnlander with long big fingers that had yellowish black nicotine all over them. He was so lazy his wife would cut the wood except when my Dad went over and had a talk to him about that. All I ever saw him do was smoke those roll your owns. Even his long teeth were black from smoking. The women here could not move even if they wished to, because where would they go?

Mr. Rydell was English and in our eyes very rich because he owned a team of horses along with two cows plus two pigs and a few chickens. They lived just south of Victor the Finn Lander in a large house. Mrs. Rydell was not seen very often as she did all the daily chores. Her husband was old Gus. They had a son around eighteen, about all he could do was drive a team of horses. They had a daughter my brother's age and she went to the same school as my brother.

Chapter Two

I recall that every spring after break up, which is when the ice has left the lake open for travel, we would welcome Jim Chief and his wife Tootimah when they paddled in and made camp just below the falls. They got dry poles that they cut from the bush, and set up a teepee with a canvas for a floor.

As it happened my dad was home for a few days from the bush camp. He came outside and asked if I would like to meet Jim Chief and his wife Tootimah. Of course I jumped at the offer. We started off to the waterfalls. We went across the tracks and a short distance away were the waterfalls, which had rocks and old timbers that had been there since the mill had shut down. The endless gush of water had the same sound constantly. After you have heard it for a long time it seemed as though it was not there. I noticed that as we drew closer to the falls our voices would automatically get louder. That waterfall would be there long, long, after we're gone. We can only keep the memory. I still remember the old bridge across the top of the falls to the other side. That is where Jim Chief had his teepee set up.

Dad said the bridge was some thirty years old and was still safe to cross by foot. So we walked across. There, below on the shore, was Jim Chief waving his arms in greeting. He lifted the teepee flap and motioned to Tootimah and pointed at us coming down the embankment.

As we approached closer I saw them for the first time. The two stood with out-stretched arms looking at my dad. They both had an Indian fashioned greeting, where Jim said something in Indian to dad while clasping his hand and arm. He nodded toward Tootimah, and she responded with a nod. Jim Chief then asked us to sit on a log close to their fire, which had a few steel black pots turned upside down. Dad had not coached me in any of the protocol, so I just kept quiet until told otherwise. I was pretty excited. In fact I felt as though I needed to go to the bathroom, but I didn't.

My dad came over and said in a low voice: "Just sit still and I will call you when you will meet them."

My dad had been invited to sit with them on a large piece of firewood, between Jim Chief and Tootimah. I could not make out what they were talking about but it seemed to me that they talked for a good long time.

Then my dad approached me with Jim on his side, and said to Jim: "This is my youngest son John." I stood up and Jim Chief took my hand into both of his. I shall never forget when I looked into his eyes. They were crystal clear and beautiful brown in a setting that felt very comfortable to look into. His face did not match, as it was the color of tree bark wrinkled from age. His forehead was the same, furrowed. His ears were even wrinkled. His hands when he grasped mine felt soft and warm, so trusting. He was about mother's height: five foot three, and thin. I could not see his hair as he wore a deer-skin hat with a brim. I found out that Tootimah had made it for him. His smile showed blackish teeth top and bottom, but very short. Perhaps they were shortened from long wear. He wore knee-high moccasins, deer-skin pants, and a shirt. He gave off a radiance of good feeling. Jim Chief was old, real old.

As he held my hand he was mumbling something I could not understand. Dad interrupted by leaning over to me: "He's saying an Indian prayer for you."
In his broken English it seemed like he kept his teeth together. "Show dish is your young boy. You look very healthy." Then he took one hand and put it on top of my head. I felt the warmth of his hand and it was comforting. He then turned and sat down beside my dad. This was my first

introduction to Jim Chief — the great legend that dad had talked about many times.

Meanwhile Tootimah looked like a person in a Halloween costume. That was my first impression. The surprising thing was that when she looked at me there was some kind of loving connection that felt comforting. I was going to greet her but dad motioned for me to sit where I was. Tootimah went over and fixed the fire adding another stick of wood. She walked around and picked up a pail for water and then she started to walk down to the bottom of the falls to fill it up. I made a motion to help; however, dad raised his hand for me to sit while he kept talking to Jim Chief. Tootimah came back with the water pail full of water. She had walked down an incline to get the water, flipped the pail and scooped up the water. Being so frail in so many ways I wondered where she got the strength from to carry that heavy pail all the way back up to the fire — seemingly without effort on her part. Amazing, I thought - she had arms like slender twigs — you had to see it to believe it. She was a small frail woman with small twig like arms, hunchbacked, with nimble strong legs. She hardly raised her head to look what she was doing.

I sat there hoping dad would finish his visit with Jim because I had to ask him about Tootimah's unusual strength.

Dad suddenly stood up, nodded to Jim Chief and motioned for me to come along.

To reach the road home we had to go up an embankment, which was rocky with clay that was dry. I made it without help. And all the while I thought about Tootimah coming up the embankment from below the falls carrying a twenty-five pound pail of water and weighing only about a hundred pounds herself. We reached the top of the embankment and dad was off at a fast pace, which made me almost run so I didn't have a chance to talk to him. There were so many questions I wanted to find out about but I would have to ask them later. I guess for that reason everything stayed with me as an imprint in my mind for a future time. I had never been inside a school-room, so I had no idea about writing. My best and only method was by remembering by the miracle of mind photography and automatically press my mental "save button" and I could recall it for a lifetime. Of course I did not know I had the most modern built-in computer that never needed a bigger memory card.

Chapter Three

When we arrived home, mother was waiting to hand dad a letter that had been delivered by a man from the railroad section crew that checked the tracks daily. Each crew along the way passes important mail to the next crew to deliver. Dad looked at the letter and went over to Mr. Rydell's house for him to read it. Dad could not read English very well.

We could see dad as he was walking back home with a smile on his face, holding the letter. Mother went and opened the door and dad sat down on a kitchen chair.

"Well," he said, "Mama you will have running water and an electric washing machine because we have a house in town. Johnny, you will go to school this fall." "Yippee," I shouted as I gave mom a big hug. We did a dance. My heart was pounding. I was overpowered with joy as I jumped on dad's knee to give him a hug. "When? When?" I kept asking.

Dad put the letter on the table and turned to mom, saying, "We have our house and I will get a ride into town when the section crew comes back in a few hours. I will get things arranged and our son Ernie will help me. In the meantime, you and

Johnny can start to pack using the boxes I have put into the wood shed."

Looking at me, he said: "You be the man in the house and help your mother with what ever she wants. Will you?" He asked. "Yes, yes," I responded. "One more thing Johnny," said dad. "Go over and check out Jim Chief and Tootimah's camp site." He said he was going to pack up and go into town for his supplies.

Next morning I had a yearning to go and check out the campsite. Dad had left for town in the late afternoon with the section crew. He had a place to stay, with a friend at his home. In the meantime I was on my way across the bridge to the campsite.

I went down the sharp incline to the place they had camped. I could not believe what I saw. Not one indent in the ground where the teepee had stood. No sign of a fire, such as ashes or burned sticks and where did the rocks go that surrounded the fire. It was like there never had been anyone ever been there. I recall feeling very confused. How could this be possible? It was, because I was standing right where it should have been, but it wasn't there. That is all I could tell dad when I saw him.

Suddenly, in a very few days we were going to move away from my childhood home. It was the only place in the world that I knew. I thought about the fact that Jim Chief and Tootimah knew plenty about moving from one place to another. They could do it without even leaving a trace. We had to pack our furniture, clothes, dishes, and God only knows what else. I did not know even where to help. I recall going to mother, grabbing her apron, I cried. The unknown really scared me.

Mother came to the rescue, telling me that dad had gone into town to get us a place to live. She said that I would stay at the same place my brother was staying at, for the time being. She and dad would get all the household goods packed up and ready to go into our new house. She also told me that dad had been looking at a house for some time and finally he would buy it. They had saved up enough money, she said.

Chapter Four

It was a time of confusion but I found a playmate by the name of Cliff. He was my age and he accepted me although I couldn't speak very much English. He said I would learn. I never forgot that he accepted me as I was. Of course mother and dad were both loving and very kind. Dad made a pair of skis for each of us from some birch logs that he let dry for a year. He had brought the logs when we moved. They were nice and light. He also made two sleighs, one for each of us. The Christmas we moved into town he bought both of us a pair of skates and hockey sticks. Dad was a trapper of wild animals for their skins that he sold for our livelihood. We always had an abundance of wild meat to eat: deer, moose, partridge, and fish that dad smoked. Mother canned all the wild meat that she put into glass sealers. We always had a good winter supply. He also built a Finnish Sauna bath which we used twice a week. Mother would always come in and scrub our ears and then tap our face with a birch leaf crop called a vita (in finnish). This was to remove acne from my face by taping it on my back. I never had a blemish on my facial skin.

I was seven when we moved into town. I recall holding mother's hand when we walked down the main street with stores and people. There were twenty five hundred people in the town. I was to start school in a short time and I did not know how to speak much English. But I still felt a bit like an ethnic misfit, very low on the ladder when it came to understanding the main accepted language. My friend Cliff and I felt like we were lower classmen, although all the children were all in the same boat. They were English, French, Swedish, Finnish, Ukrainian and Chinese. There wasn't much point in socializing because we couldn't understand each other anyway. You can imagine sitting in a classroom with this mixture of tongues.

Chapter Five

Each year we always had a visit, once in the spring, once in the fall, from our dear old friends, namely, Tootimah and Jim Chief. Arriving home one day after school in early September I saw, to my great surprise, that Jim Chief had pitched his tent in our back yard, on the lawn part, as the rest was garden. The flap of the tent opened and there stood Jim Chief, out-stretching his hand to greet me, with his face smile and kind eyes. I took his hand and immediately felt a comforting transmission of kindness and love. I had never had this experience before. He had the same hat with a feather sticking from the hatband. "How is the young schoolboy today?" he said in his broken English. "Fine Mr. Chief," I answered and went into the house to see mother and dad.

Then my brother came in behind me, asking, "What is Jim Chief doing camped in our yard?" "He wants to stay close to us for a few days, before he goes back into the bush for the winter," my dad answered. He also told us that Jim Chief and Tootimah were not coming back next spring. "Why?" My brother asked. Dad looked at my brother and said, "Tootimah is now getting very old so she has made up her mind that she is going to a place in the bush, that she has chosen, will lie down and let herself die.

"She has not even told Jim Chief where that place is that she has chosen. Jim told me that if he does not come back next spring that he would be camping on the trap line. And he said that when I go to see him, I am to bring you along because he has a gift for you. I am also to pick-up the regular supplies that they need. I know what he needs. We will go in May next year because he told me that there would be very much rain in April."

"And oh yes," Dad said, "The reason he is going to camp on my trap line is because the snowfall in the winter will be light."

Jim Chief stayed in our yard for three more days and then one morning he and Tootimah were gone. The tent and all their belongings had vanished. My brother and I went out to take a look. I remembered once again what I had seen by the falls where we had lived. Not a blade of grass out of place. It was amazing and unbelievable. The yard was left so clean like no one had been there. What fabulous people they were, so rich in spirit and love. No hindrance to society not even in their own death, everything was so harmonious within themselves. They had total acceptance and reliance in their maker and master.

When I got back into the house, dad asked me to come into the living room and sit down for a talk.

Dad sat across from me in his chair. "Well, son," he said, "You and I have been asked by Jim Chief to meet with him next spring. He wants to meet with you so that he can pass on some of his methods like carrying a canoe filled with supplies over the distance of a one-mile portage. That will be both up and down a rocky path where you can put the canoe down into safe water."

I wanted to know why Jim Chief was willing to pass on these great secrets of lifting heavy weights plus walking through bush without effort. "Did he say exactly when?" "Yes, dad answered, "the week after you are finished school."

My mind started to whirl around imagining myself carrying an eight hundred-pound canoe from the bottom of a waterfall to the top so that we could continue our journey. So this is a method Jim Chief's ancestors used to transport large quantities of firs and supplies in short periods of time. "It is a good time now my son for you to keep this to yourself because that is the way Jim Chief would want it," dad said. "Surely I can tell my best friend like Cliff, so that I can talk about it," I reasoned. "Only the two of you because if Jim Chief knows he will not pass it on to you and you will make the choice." I did not mention anything to Cliff at this time.

Chapter Six

Dad was waiting for me outside the school grounds to walk me home. I remembered when I was younger he used to put me on his shoulders so that I got a ride home. It felt so good. I was now too big at the age of twelve. As we walked Dad talked while he carried my heavy load of books because we were now finished school for the summer. I had just cleaned out my desk.

Leisurely walking along, Dad came out with the blockbuster. "We are going to meet with Jim Chief a few miles down the English River," he announced. "Jim will be in that area for awhile." I just about dropped my books, saying; "Jim Chief's timing is perfect — and what is he going to show me?" "We will let him tell us about that when we meet him," dad answered.

My mind was racing with thoughts zooming from one thing to another and not making any sense. I had tried to study a little about ancient times. I learned the Incas of South America had developed and built pyramid-type monuments using heavy rock. They were, apparently, aligned perfectly with compass bearings. Along with all of these wondrous things I wondered whether Jim Chief was related to these Indians in some past time. I was curious: where did he come from, where was he born, what tribe, how and when did he receive these gifts? Or was he born with them? They were miraculous with out a doubt. I had a hard time trying to sleep. I did, however, fall asleep as I quieted myself and relaxed.

The first voice I heard in the morning was that of mother as she said to come for breakfast. I was excited as I washed and got my clothes on that mother had ready for me. Dad had already gone. I finnished a good big bowl of porridge and was on my way.

Down at the boathouse dad put our gear into the boat. I untied the boat, gave it a shove out, and we were on our way. Dad gave the engine a pull and it came to life.

The day was calm where you could see the reflection of the shoreline with the trees and shore in an upside-down position in the mirror-like crystal clear water. Birds were using the slight wind to glide along in the air. There was complete peace and serenity. So this is the world of the Great Universal Intelligence! Who couldn't say thanks to that? It felt like I was in a wonderful trance when dad announced that we were not very far away from Jim Chief's camp. Dad motioned with his finger that it was just around the point of land ahead.

Chapter Eight

As the boat turned slowly around the point you could see smoke and a small fire. There they were: Tootimah and Jim Chief. Jim came down and guided the boat on to the shore. I jumped out as dad's weight brought the bow of the boat up so I could secure it to the shore.

Jim Chief took my hand and shook it in welcome not speaking but looking into my eyes with a smile as he said: "Welcome with your dad to my home."

"Thank you very much," I responded as dad said something in Indian as a greeting. We then proceeded up to the campfire where Tootimah was already sitting on the ground and Jim came and sat beside her. I noticed when he sat down that he had a feather placed on one side of his black hat. He took his hat off and started to stroke the feather looking up and moving his lips in silence. Tootimah kept her eyes on him and would mutter back to him once or twice nodding her head.

The silence was broken when Jim started to talk. It felt like everything was quiet as he began in his broken English. We had to listen carefully because his Indian thinking was faster than his interpretation back to English. He had to repeat because it didn't come out like he wanted it to. I sat with my legs crossed on the ground just opposite Jim and Tootimah. Dad sat on a dry stump.

"Dad has told me about the many great things about you," I said. "He told me that you could carry an eight hundred-pound canoe over a long portage."

"Yes, I can do that," Jim Chief said. "Your father knows the great Chiefs of long, long, ago passed the secrets to only a few of us. I believe I am the only one left that is alive with these gifts that were given to me. There are only certain people that can do this but many were shown. The gifts came from an old Indian tribe that lived far, far away to the south in the other America. I will be going to the happy hunting ground soon," Jim continued, "and I would like to pass it on to one of your dad's sons. He has always been so good to Tootimah and myself."

I jumped in. "Please Mr. Chief, will you show me this ancient power?"

"Hold on!" My dad motioned. "You must wait for Jim to ask you, if he so wishes."

Looking at me directly, Jim said: "You said the magic word. That is 'power'. Our great chiefs stopped using these secrets a long time ago.

24

They lost the power because they gave it away in order to better themselves. The power did very much good because they built many great places of worship and burial tombs. As more people got to know how to use this power, then most of the men that had this power began to think of themselves as the sole owners of the gifts. They began to think of themselves as 'The Great Spirit'. The moment this thinking developed, they lost the gifts. Their privilege was taken away."

I interrupted by saying the people worshipped them like gods as they took over as rulers of the land.

"You're a very smart young boy," Jim said, "Maybe you will be the one I can give this gift to — if you want it."

"Do I want it? Of course I want to have it. That is if dad says OK."

"Yes and we will follow Jim's rules," said dad.

"Your father can bring you to my tent up further up the river. He can leave you with me for a few days so that I can teach you all the things that you can someday pass on to another person that you will choose. You will not have to worry who it will be because the Great Spirit will tell you. The same way that he told me that you were to be the one."

Jim Chief lifted up his head and gazed into the sky. Then he said: "I will meet you at the old mill falls early next month when the moon is full. Your father will bring you. The weather will be good. Maybe your father can bring your tent for the overnight stay."

There was a tremendous feeling of a surge of energy came in and through me like a blanket it covered me with warmth. This elation was a total feeling serenity and joy. I kept watch the moon as it slowly got bigger, with the trip to the old mill constantly on my mind. How had Jim known, without a calendar, the exact time the moon would be full? What kind of a built-in time, day, and weather calculator did he have? He did all of this instantly right on the spot.

Chapter Nine

It was early morning when dad awakened me saying the time had come he would take me to Jim Chief's place at the Old Mill. "The moon was full after midnight last night, so we have to be on our way," he said.

I made sure that I put on warm clothes. Mother had a big breakfast ready for us both, plus hot coffee for dad and a large glass of orange juice for me. She already had a lunch packed in a wooden lunch box with leather strap for a handle.

I went over to mother and gave her a hug and a kiss on the cheek and left with dad on our way to the boathouse.

Dad had filled up the gas cans and gathered all the supplies in the boat. The trip to the Old Mill was quite a distance up the river. I gave the boat a push with a paddle and it glided out onto the lake. When all was clear dad gave the engine a crank as it sprang to life. He throttled up speed and we were off. The shoreline of trees and rock looked as though the rock had been cut with a laser saw. We veered close to the rocky shore. I looked up and the rock cliff was at least fifteen feet high and straight up. I knew from the past, that fishing was very good in this deep water for lake trout. Looking east, the morning sun was glittering on the calm water while the birds that recently took flight for their morning breakfast hovered above. I was looking ahead with great anticipation as to what I was going to learn in the next few days with Jim Chief.

I dozed off with the hum of the boat engine. The boat suddenly started to slow down and woke up. We were already coming close to shore. "That was fast," I quipped.

"Yes," said dad. "You never even woke up when I stopped to add gas to the tank an hour ago. But that's O.K. you will be well awake for Jim and Tootimah.They should be here in about ten minutes."

Dad pointed the boat to a sandy part of the beach. It landed with a thud. I stepped out and the bow of the boat rose up from dad's weight at the back. I pulled the boat up as far as I could and Dad got out.

"Where will they come from?" I asked.

Chapter Ten

"We have been waiting for you," Jim Chief announced suddenly from beside a large Jack Pine tree. "You fellows are right on time. We will make a fire and have some good tea."

Dad was sure right because Jim Chief showed up from nowhere with Tootimah. This was awesome. It happened as though it was normal. Baffling, but normal.

Tootimah had a large tin can with a piece of wire for a handle. She took it down to the lake for fresh water. Jim Chief fixed a place for the fire. Dad gathered some kindling along with birch bark to start the fire. Tootimah placed the handle of the can on the end of a stick, which Jim had placed while dad lit the fire.

I could hear the waterfalls in the distance. The birch, jack pine and spruce trees were absolutely straight and all surrounded with beautiful green grass with moss on the tree trunks. Then in the background were huge Tamarack trees standing like guards each in strategic positions. Their bark looked like armor plating. It was so peaceful and the trees gave a slight sway at the top from the breeze.

Dad came close and announced to me that it was time for lunch. We go by Jim's rules here; we will only eat after he has started.

"Where is Jim's lunch?" I asked dad.

"You will see," he said.

Shortly, Jim announced the tea was ready. Dad brought up the cups from the boat and held them out for Jim to pour.

I took a sip which I almost spit out because it was like tar and as black as a telephone. It was Indian tea courtesy of Jim Chief. Made by a real Indian.

It seemed like we sat for a long time sipping that black tea. I had to sip because a mouthful at a time I would have had to spit it out. No one spoke just looking out at the river. I made a move to stand when dad nudged me to sit.

When Jim finished his tea, he asked me to get the minnow net and scoop some minnows to catch fish for us to eat. The minnow net was a small mesh net. Dad had made a wire hoop attached fish netting attached to a wooden pole.

I went down picked up the net and walked over to the rocks. I could not believe it because there were hundred of minnows swimming around. I scooped out once with the net, put them into the minnow pail. I took my fishing rod, with hook on, out of the boat, ready to go. I threaded the minnow onto the hook and cast it into the slight current. Low and behold I had a strike with a good catch on. I brought the fish in and landed it on the shore. I put some more bait on and cast it out. Wow! I had another one on the line. There was fish number two, which, on top of what mom had packed earlier, was more than enough for our meal. I gave them to dad so that he could clean them.

Jim reminded me to go down and put the other minnows back into the water, because we did not need them. When I went back down to where I had scooped them out I looked into the crevice and there was not a minnow in sight. They were just there to meet our needs for the meal.

The meal was ready with some sourdough bread that we had brought plus fresh butter. We ate slowly and very quietly. Everything felt in order. When we were finished, dad stood up and said to me: "This is the last time that you will have fish fried in a pan for awhile because Jim and Tootimah have their own way of cooking. You will find out in the next two days that you are here, because I am taking everything back, except your sleeping bag, tent, and pack of clothes. There is extra tea, sugar and flour for Jim and Tootimah. I will see you back here in two days." As he started to walk down to the boat, dad turned to me and said: "You will learn some great secrets from Jim and Tootimah that will be with you for your lifetime."

There were no formal handshakes or hugs. I just helped him get the boat back into the water. Jim stood on the shore, with his arms folded, gazing out towards dad mouthing something. The engine started and with a wave dad was on his way. I started to feel homesick already because I had not been away from mom and dad ever.

Chapter Eleven

Jim broke my stare when he said, "I can call you Onni's son John. That way we will know for sure whom we are talking to or asking the Great Power to help. The Great Power knows your dad. You will get to know many things that will no longer be strange to you, such as, carrying a heavy canoe, walking in the bush and making no noise and you will be shown how to do things that you thought were impossible. You will live a good life."

He said Tootimah would look after the campfire and have everything back in place I took my backpack and went along with him. And sure enough as I turned I saw Tootimah as she effortlessly cleaned the camping spot with a willow branch by waving it back and forth. I could not believe my eyes as everything moved back to the way it had been. This how they cleaned up our back yard when they camped there. I moved swiftly to be behind Jim.

"We will find a quiet place," Jim continued, "where we can become one with the surroundings. We will feel together as with the forest and land. You do not have to remember what you have learned in the white man's school. You are going to find your other inner self."

I struggled walking through the bush behind Jim as he walked effortlessly as though walking on a path without hitting any branches. He seemed to jump from rock to rock like hopscotch. I already had scrapes on my arms from short branches. I then noticed Tootimah right behind me as though I was holding her up. I was going to say to her to go ahead but thought better because I didn't want to lose them.

We were walking along a ridge of a slope moving upwards as we went. I could hear the sound of waterfalls louder but did not know where it was coming from.

Jim turned and said we were almost at our camping place. "We will go up this side." He pointed from where he stood and said: "There is our place for the next two days. You can put your tent up under that big jackpine tree. It will be nice and dry for you with no wind." I followed Jim down to the big tree where I put my pack down, thankfully. Jim had his tent closer to the water where Tootimah had already arrived.

I took my tent bag to the spot under the tall pine tree where Jim had suggested that I pitch my tent. I had set the tent up several times so that it was not a chore that I was concerned about because it would only take me about a half-hour to complete. I got busy.

While I worked I could hear all the sounds, the birds, the wind through the trees, the chirping of squirrels; a fish would jump up in the small river as well as the waterfalls further up. All I had left to do was get some spruce bows for my mattress and then open my sleeping bag with a small pillow and it was ready to sleep in. I went into the bush and found a nice short log, which I could sit on.

The log was ideal as I rested on it and gazed about seeing all of the lush beauty. Again I saw the pipe organ like trees with the colors of birch bark, willow of light gray, the green of the huge spruce trees, then the crystal clear water of the small river that glistened in the daylight. I felt in awe as I saw Jim coming up towards my tent.

You have a nice dry place, which is out of the wind, and when you lie down to sleep the noise of the falls will not be bad because when you are close to the ground you will hardly hear it. Thank you Jim, my tent looked like a small teepee.

All of a sudden Jim was standing beside me, I interrupted the silence with a slight cough. "We will go down to the falls," said Jim, "there is a nice place to sit and talk."

I nodded and followed him.

Amazingly, as Jim walked ahead of me he made no sound on the twigs or leaves. He seemed to float over the ground with each step. The bush seemed alive with sounds of birds with a crow high overhead cawing, then a flock of ducks all in perfect formation going further north while looking for a good feeding stop. A few fish were jumping which seemed like they were playing in the waterfalls.

Chapter Thirteen

When we arrived at Jim's designated spot, he lifted up both arms and spread his hands over the water and the land. His palms were facing flat to the water as he began to speak with his eyes wide open looking at the water. Swaying from one side to the other in muffled perhaps Indian.

Then all of a sudden he began to speak in his broken English. "Oh Great Spirit of the Universe. I bring to You a young man that in my heart is worthy to hand over the great Gift that You have allowed me to have. Thank you for allowing me to have this Gift which You had my brother give to me many years ago. I am now old and have only two hunting seasons left for me to be here. Tootimah is going after the next season. She is giving You thanks from our camp now. I will pass the Great Secret prayer to Onni's son so that he to can lift great weights the same way You had builders of the past build places with large stones as well as heavy equipment like You gave me. I will now sit and wait for Your approval of Onni's son in my mind."

There was a silence and quietness; not even the waterfalls made any sound. It seemed like there was no rustle of leaves as Jim waited. He stared intensely into the crystal clear water then he slowly lifted his arms in the same manner as he had before and said: "Thank you." He had received His message.

It was like waiting for your teacher to tell you if you passed. Jim looked at me and nodded his head in approval. I felt as though a great burden had been lifted from me. And I was washed over with a sense of peace and serenity. Jim motioned for me to come and sit beside him. The ground was like a carpet of dry moss. Both of us sat cross-legged and faced the water.

Jim started to talk and I could hear him loud and clear when he said to me. "Do you believe in the great trees, water, land, and the Great Spirit made all that is therein."

"Yes I do," I answered.

I felt an inner joy as though a new force had entered me without any effort on my part. This experience was something I had never witnessed before. It was a feeling of attachment to all the surroundings. The place was giving Jim Chief an insurmountable amount of energy. I felt this power surge in and through me, too. I now knew that I was having a spiritual experience.

Jim interrupted my thoughts as he said: "Does it feel like soft bubbles floating around inside of you and making you feel good?"

"Yes, yes that is it. That is the way I feel," I said. "I feel as though I am one with everything and have the feeling of being loved. I feel as though I have learned more than is possible, just by being here."

"You now have inner wisdom," Jim said. "What you have been given is a gift from the Creator. Everyone and everything that is on this land is here for a purpose. Every one, human, animal, water, is in its proper place, nothing happens by mistake. It is all a part of the great design that has been planned and is for our use. I will now take you to my canoe, which is just around this point of land." He lifted up his hand to show the way.

Chapter Fourteen

We walked slowly and it seemed effortless as I moved my feet. I felt lighter as though I was walking above the ground. We both walked in silence; not even a twig broke the silence. I felt as though I was acquiring the same ability that Jim had. I could now walk without making a sound on the ground I broke the silence to Jim, who was ahead of me and said; "I am walking without making a sound, the same as you."

"I know you are," Jim answered.

We arrived at the canoe and Jim asked me to just stand and watch. Jim moved from the stern to the bow of the canoe mouthing something to him and then turned to me and said: "What you will now see, you will not believe is possible." He then continued: "This canoe is loaded with supplies plus outboard motor and the gasoline cans that are full. Out of the water it must weigh at least six hundred pounds. I will take this canoe and make it as light as air, put it on my shoulders with the bottom resting on my back. I will carry the loaded canoe up and over the falls to the clear water up there …" He pointed up to the top of the falls.

Jim walked to the middle of the loaded canoe and stroked the gunwale. He muttered words I could not understand and then with his hand on the side began to lift and up came the canoe as though it defied gravity; it was light in his hands. He placed the keel on his shoulders. He walked leisurely along the footpath that had been made by others as they carried their gear along the same path. It was truly astounding as I was seeing something unbelievable.

Now I knew how they could build pyramids in Egypt and large palaces in South America. No wonder they could move huge pieces of granite without any modern equipment. I had witnessed a miracle. I followed Jim to the top of the falls as he set the canoe down on the shoreline where a launching area had been made. Jim looked at me and said it saves a lot of hard work carrying each piece up here. "I am now going to show you how to do this and bring the canoe back down to where we started," he said. "Come here close to me because you already have the feeling, right?"

"Right," I answered.

"Now," Jim continued, "you are going to talk to your innermost self as you say these words that I will tell you. Remember them because they are in the Indian language. He put his head to my ear and said the words. I nodded in agreement. I knew I would not forget them, even though it was in Indian."

I walked to the bow of the canoe, then walked to the middle repeating what he had told me. I took the gunnel with one hand sliding the other to the bottom and slowly started to lift. The canoe moved effortlessly with the keel on my shoulder the same way as Jim had done. I looked at Jim as a great smile of appreciation came over us both. I walked the canoe on my shoulder to the botton of the falls.

Jim motioned to sit with him on a couple of rocks. He said we could now sit here and be truly thankful and grateful for the great gift that was given to us. We sat in silence.

Chapter Fifteen

You must remember that Jim said the energy force that surrounds you gives this gift to you. You must always get that feeling and ability down deep within your self. It will only come to you when you are surrounded with trees and plants. It will not work for you with other people around or if there is man made noise. I can't tell you how long you will keep it. Do not use it for the purpose of other people knowing you have this gift. Eventually the spirit will tell to find another person to give it to. It will be in your end times.

"My time is coming one year after Tootimah," Jim said. "Tootimah will go for her end-time walk next fall where she will find a good place to rest. You will know these things and accept them in your heart. I have now completed my duties," Jim said as he got up from the rock where he sat.

We started the walk back to our campsite and I queried Jim by asking how he knew Tootimah would go next fall.

"She has already picked her spot where she will go," Jim replied. "Remember this, it is our custom that when we grow old and unable to do things for ourselves that we find a comfortable place that we like. The spirit will come and take her soul away to the happy hunting grounds. It is our duty to do this."

As we walked back to our tent Jim invited me to his camp for a meal. "You come now Onni's son to our tent and have food with us we are both hungry and Tootimah will have it ready for us.

"Thank you Jim," I responded.

Chapter Sixteen

We arrived at Jim and Tootimah's camp as she was preparing the meal. I had no idea what we were going to eat. She had prepared two short pieces of a dry log for Jim and I to sit on. It was very picturesque with the clear crystal river just down from the embankment and tall pine trees standing like guards. The air felt clean and pure that it almost had a taste to it. Each breath felt as though it went in and through you. She had stacked the wood onto the fire in the same shape as the teepee with three black pots on sticks, each with a support a quarter of the way up to control how close to the fire she wanted each pot. The pots were covered so there was no peaking at the food. One problem was that the odor was not gourmet, more like boiled fish. The weather was calm and it was getting into the late afternoon. We sat in silence except for Tootimah who moved about doing her chores; she also walked about without making any noise only the crackle of the campfire. They had silent moccasins.

Jim stood up and went over to their tent and came over with three wooden bowls, handing one to me. It looked like it had been carved out of a piece of birch wood. It was well shaped and easy to hold.

Jim then said: "Most white men like to wash their hands before they eat so you can go down to the river. You will see some dry moss and it will dry your hands. I will put some food into your bowl."

He was right because I washed my hands in water that swirled around in a small eddy of rock, like an automatic hand washer, really refreshing. The dry moss just seemed to massage my hands dry. And then I went back up for my surprise meal.

Jim had my bowl ready as I approached and he handed it to me saying: "This is a special meal that is made when we pass on a gift like you have been given. It is in honor of the Great Spirit. It is made from various roots and fish. You will have to add salt if you choose but it is sweet to our taste."

"Thank you," I said, "but do you have a spoon?"

"We only use the bowl and you can use your fingers to eat the meat and the rest you can drink."

"Thanks," I said.

Jim gave me a full bowl of Tootimah's special meal along with some bannock. Bannock is a type of Indian bread that is like hard tack that you have to soak in liquid. I broke off a chunk and threw it into the soup when Jim told me that we could only dunk it and not let it soak. I fished mine out with my fingers and had a taste. What a surprise! The liquid tasted sweet and tangy, not sugar sweet but a different kind of herb sweet. It was delicious. Now I had to grasp a piece of fish by a bone, which brought up a piece of backbone and some good meat. Again the taste was superb. No chef could ever match Tootimah's fish stew. It reminded me of coconut shrimp soup. I sat on the log with my legs apart so as not to spill food. Jim said: "Don't be afraid of some food on your clothes because animals don't like the smell of this food so they will stay away." I asked Jim for another bowl, which he gave me with a closed mouth smile. I just thought he was shy of his teeth because they were so black. I brought the bowl up to my mouth and sipped the liquid, which again tasted so delicious. I noticed birds and hawks circling above because Jim threw the bones toward the river. The birds swooped down as soon as the bones hit the ground. Jim and Tootimah never paid any attention to the birds or the squirrels that were busy. I finished my second bowl and said thanks.

To my surprise Tootimah said: "You like my mulligan?"

"Yes, very much," I said. She had a smile that displayed a few black teeth. She had nice eyes. We finished the meal and made our way to the river and washed out our bowls, which we dried with the moss.

There was no conversation as we made our way back to the campsite and sat down in our spots with Tootimah sitting beside Jim, on the ground. She sat cross-legged on the soft moss for a cushion.

Jim opened the conversation because dad had told me not to start talking until Jim was ready to speak.

Jim raised his arms with his palms facing upwards to the sky. He looked straight up. He spoke in a babble of tongues. Slowly he relaxed himself while Tootimah also had her frail arms up above her head and followed along with Jim.

I watched them both as the campfire was slowly burning itself out with a small stream of smoke going straight up into the calm air as the day started to cool down. The bush was quiet except for a loon at the bottom of the waterfalls. Peace and quiet permeated all about us. It was very comforting.

Jim broke the silence by saying, "Tootimah and I are very proud of you. You are now just like us in the eyes of the Great Spirit. The meal was the final part of the ceremony for you receiving the gift for as long as you shall live. Tootimah will take you in the morning to show you the proper roots that will be needed to put into the mulligan."

As the sky was starting to fade Jim came over and said: "In a little while the sun will give every one a rest for the night and we will be up at sunrise. You make yourself comfortable with a good sleep until morning."

Jim turned and went inside his tent and I walked over to mine. I unrolled the sleeping bag and took off my pants, leaving my shirt on. I rolled a part of the sleeping bag a little for a pillow. My day, as I recounted the happenings were just to much to be able to go through so I just said a part of the prayer Jim had told me. The next thing I knew Jim was hitting two pieces of wood together and I woke up. The sun was starting to come up in the east. I just acknowledged Jim by saying thanks.

Tootimah had already put water on for tea. Jim said we would have some tea to warm us and Tootimah made some breakfast mulligan would keep us going until dad arrived. "Tootimah will take you along the river to show you the plant roots, which you will know, after she shows you," said Jim. "Here is some tea."

I took the wooden bowl of tea and had a sip. It was hot and so strong I felt I had to chew it. I managed to drink the entire bowl and that took me awhile. Jim rinsed the same bowl and ladled some of the breakfast mulligan into it.

I was surprised by how good it tasted. It had a sweet taste like our white cooking coconut. It was stringy but very rich, most certainly different and good.

Jim looked over at me and said: "You will be going to what you call the outhouse pretty soon after we have eaten. This will clean you out." He smiled in a way that again showed his black teeth. I thought to myself that drinking that Indian tea would make anybody's teeth black. I wondered how my teeth were with only a few cups. There was no mirror to look into.

Chapter Seventeen

Tootimah came over to me and pulled on my shirt cuff to come along with her. I followed her as she went through the bush not even moving a branch and surprisingly I was doing the same thing. We came to a stop and she muttered in Indian when she pointed at a small plant that I know to this day as well as four others plus the leaves of a willow tree. She nudged my arm and pointed towards the river. I looked and saw a big black bear with his head eyeing the water and then like a flash he had his paw in the water and out came a large size fish that the bear threw onto the shore. He got up out of the water and went over to where the fish was. He started to eat it and had it all eaten up in a matter of minutes and went down to the river to do some more fishing. I noticed that the bear only ate one fish at a time because he would know when he had enough to eat. There was no waste of food. I noticed Tootimah slowly nodding her head with a smile on her wrinkled, weather-beaten face. Her face looked like a piece of fine leather that turned into a smile. Beautiful I thought.

We seemed to both turn at the same time to go back to the campsite. Tootimah never walked ahead but followed behind me. I felt honored because she always walked behind Jim. I walked with a different gait, confident and reassured in a new confident way. I felt older than I was.

When we arrived, Jim was sitting on his short log chair looking toward us and motioning for me to sit on my seat. "Now you know the right roots and plants to use when you make the mulligan. You will not have to remember them because the Great Spirit will remind you where and what to look for."

"Thank-you very much to the both of you for each and every gift you have so graciously given to me," I said.

"You are welcome," said Jim. "Now I want you to kneel in front of Tootimah and me so that we can make this all right with our Great Spirit. Take your cap off so that we can both put our hands on top of your head."

There was a feeling of warmth and slowly it felt as if a slight electrical pulse moved down my spine and filtered throughout my body. It was like a massage performed from the inside. Jim and Tootimah started to chant. It reminded me of religious tongues that I had read about. They both stopped as though on cue. I heard Jim's voice as he said in his own broken English: "Take this man into your heart oh Great Spirit as we ask you to guide him in the ways of this great land. Give him his daily food, health, rest and wisdom. Let him awaken each day with the newness of Your Plan that You have made for us each day. Guide him to follow that plan and not his own. Protect him as he leaves today with his dad." They both lifted their hands off of my head but the feeling still lingered. Jim then said; "You could go and get your tent and bed ready to leave because when you are finished you will hear the kicker (motor) of your dad coming in his boat to get you."

Chapter Eighteen

I felt different inside and out. My whole body moved without effort, I seemed to glide to my campsite as I started to pack up my bed and tent. It was as though I was guided with each movement and everything moved perfectly into place. When the last fold was made I could hear dad's motor purring away just off shore, perhaps a mile away. It was just enough time to get over the hill to the docking area. I didn't notice Jim or Tootimah so I went alone. When I came over the hill, there they were waving at dad and he was waving back. The boat moved slowly to shore as Jim guided to a place on the sandy shore.

Jim helped dad step out of the boat and Tootimah had her thin small hand out in greeting. Her hand practically disappeared in Dad's large hand. They all patted each other on the back and dad came over to greet me with a hug. "How are you my son? You look the same as the day I gave you that new pair of skis that I had made for you."

"I have had an experience that I will never forget as long as I live, dad.

"That is very good son, but I notice Tootimah has brought a can of tea for us to sit down and enjoy. They will be going back to their campsite to eat while you and I will enjoy some sandwiches that mother made for us."

We went up and sat in our usual spots as Jim poured the tea. We drank some tea when Jim said: "This our parting drink together until we see you when you both are coming up hunting with your American friends. They will be here in the early fall before the weather changes."

"Yes, we will go to my old trapping cabin at the lake of the bays," dad said. "There will be five of us and that includes my son."

Dad and I gathered my gear and we went down to the boat to leave. I had to give Tootimah a big hug, which was almost like hugging a bundle of twigs with her frail body. But immediately I felt that tingle go through my entire body. It was great. Then I went to Jim and did the same thing and he felt just like Tootimah except for size but the same tingle through my body. It felt so good.

Chapter Nineteen

Dad was sitting at the rear as I put one foot in the boat and with the other gave a shove off. We were on our way as we looked at Tootimah and Jim Chief standing on the shore waving goodbye.

It was a clear day with sunshine and a blue sky. The air was warm except for the breeze created by the speed of the boat. We were about three miles from our departure place when dad cut the motor down and shut it off. It was quiet, calm and warm when dad said that we should talk before we got back home.

"Son, you are not to talk about what Jim Chief and Tootimah have shown you. People will not believe you. They will only make fun and ask you to show them. You can't do that as Jim explained to you. Only where you can be helpful without them knowing, such as, moving something very heavy and for a very good purpose. You will be guided when you can use your gift as Jim explained by the Great Spirit."

I asked inquisitively; "Did Jim give you the secret gift?"

"Even if he did I could not tell you because the secret gift is secret and only the person that has it knows. If you have it only you know by yourself," dad answered. "Now we can both go home because we feel better and can be of service to our fellow man."

When we arrived home mother was at the door to greet us. She gave me a mother hug, and then brought me in to see my sister in her special crib that dad had made for her. She didn't have a hand-me-down crib, as it was ten years between her and me. I never thought anything about age difference at that time. She was kicking and smiling as I tickled here feet. Mother turned to me and put a finger on her nose as I thought it was my sister by looking at her when mother pointed at me. I didn't realize that I had not had a bath for a few days.

Mother brought me to the kitchen door and pointed to the sauna. "I have put some clean clothes for you in there," she said. "I put the fire on this morning so will be nice and hot for you."

I undressed in the dressing room and closed the door of the sauna as I went in. I threw a wooden pitcher of water on the rocks as a burst of steam filtered out. The heat hit me with a relaxing effect then followed by sweat, which opens all the pores, which removes any body odour. This is the way you get squeaky clean. You wash your hair with ordinary soap, rinse with warm water, and it is optional to use the cold water for a rinse of your body.

When I came out of the sauna there was my best friend Cliff waiting for me with his boyish grin. I went over and put my hand on his shoulder giving him a pat. We never hugged because in our opinion, boys did not do this kind of thing. We walked over to the woodshed, which was our favorite spot. Cliff sat on a bench made very solid for a person with a wide ass as Cliff use to call it; he could bring his one leg up and lean on his knee. I sat on a small sauna stool and leaned up against the wall. He told me that he had another flat tire on his bike. The patches were cheaper than having to save for a new inner tube. We got used to fixing inner tubes. I noticed my old bike in the corner and got up to check the air and it was OK. We decided that because the next day was Sunday we could go for a ride in the morning.

Cliff was at our house bright and early ready to go riding. He said to me that my dad had told him that I was fishing with Jim Chief to which I answered, at Jim Chief's camp. "That's great," he said.

Chapter Twenty

We heard music from the church so we swung by and left our bikes in the tall grass in the ditch across the road. We listened for awhile when Cliff suggested that we take a look through the window. The window was gothic style and quite high so we had to decide who would be on top or bottom for boosting the other up. Cliff had small sticks. "Wet or dry?" he asked. "Dry" I said. He flipped it up and it landed dry. I won the toss. We always used a small stick to decide. Cliff held his hands clasped and I put one foot in and then jumped onto his shoulders. I could see the inside of the whole church. I gave a commentary to Cliff as to what was happening. "Old lady Macdonald is playing the organ," I said. "Mr. Cox (he was the minister) is wearing a long black dress. There are a whole lot of people in scarlet robes singing behind the organ."

Then all of a sudden Cliff gave my pant leg a tug and I noticed Mr.White, one of the church bosses, had come out. He yelled at us: "What are you kids doing here?" I jumped down as the two of us hit the road running. That was the only encounter we had with the church and hoped no one noticed who we were. Dad would have given us hell because we could not afford to go to church. Dad had said that if we could give them cordwood we would go. We went down the lane as we lost sight of old man White. We crept through the tall grass and got our bikes back.

One day in the summer we were sitting by the sand pit watching the wagons come down and get filled up with gravel for roads they were building in town. They only had horses to haul the wagons but they got the job done. We heard the gravel pit boss yell at us to get away and go home. First the church now the gravel pit boss all wanted us go away.

Cliff then said: "Old Jim Chief never worried about making roads and doing things like we do. He lives in the bush yet he knows more about things than most people around here do. In his world he can live happy. How come? Why don't we go and ask your dad about old Jim Chief?"

"Let's go," I said.

Chapter Twenty One

When we got home dad was in his workshop building some cupboards for mother. "What are you boys up to?" he asked.

"Cliff and I would like you to tell us about old Jim Chief because you know him so well."

Dad put his wood planer on it's side, pulled up a sauna stool, took out his Copenhagen snuff box with a tin lid, knocked with his knuckle twice, opened the lid and with his two forefingers squeezed a wad of snuff into his lower lip. "Ah," he said, "now I can think well."

Cliff asked gramps (it was OK for Cliff to call him gramps because he had asked him): "How come you tap your snuff twice before you put some in your lip?'

Dad looked at Cliff and said: "Because that way you get the fresh snuff to the top."

"Boys," he said, "If we knew what Jim Chief knew we could travel any place in the bush, summer or winter. He never worries about getting lost, finding food to eat or having a place to sleep. He knows if it will snow or rain and if the wind will blow hard. He never gets caught in a rain or snowstorm because he knows ahead of time exactly how the weather will be. Tootimah knows how to cook from roots and plants. She makes good soup. I remember one time some years ago, old Jim was in the bush when we came close to his camp on the river. I was with some Americans I was guiding on a moose-hunting trip. We pulled up to shore and all of a sudden Jim was there to guide our boat. The Americans were sure surprised to see him. One of them said: 'Where in Gods name did he come from?' 'That is Jim Chief,' I said. A couple of those Americans are going to come up this fall to hunt moose and Johnny and I will be their guides.

"Yippee," I said. "Can Cliff come along with us?"

"No," dad answered. "Because there is not enough room, Joe Dagg is going to be with us as well. Sorry Cliff."

"That's OK because you will tell me all about it when you get back," said Cliff.

"That's right," dad assured him.

I looked at Cliff and said, "Don't worry my friend you and I will get together after we get back and I will update you on exactly what happened. Is that ok?"

"Yes!" Cliff answered, "I understand that the canoes does not have any extra room. I will be thinking about you all."

When Cliff had left I asked dad when and where we would be going.

Chapter Twenty Two

"The American hunters will come here in the first week in October and leave one day after the full moon," dad said. "I'll be getting all of our supplies ready for the trip as well as the winter supplies for Jim Chief. He won't be coming in to town this fall because Tootimah is going to her hunting grounds in early winter after the full moon in the New Year."

I tried to interrupt but dad was so busy doing little odds and ends as he kept on talking

"We will go to my trapping cabin north of the English River. We have one big portage on the way so you can use your secret gift to move the canoes and supplies. You don't have to worry because I will keep the hunters busy doing some bird hunting as well as getting some fish to eat. By the way, Jim Chief and Tootimah will meet us at the lake."

Here we go again, I thought. There is well over a month to go and he gives me no exact day, exact time or even the name of the month. Yet, dad said, Jim and Tootimah would be there. This I have to see, I thought. But I couldn't hold back so I asked how could all of this come about without letting Jim Chief know.

"Well son," dad said, "when the winds change and you start to feel that cold streak, even though the sun is shining that means that I know and Jim knows that I will be on my way to my trapping cabin with my hunters one day after the full moon. I will be at the lake above the falls. Simple eh, son?"

That is exactly what happened. The hunters all arrived on schedule from the U.S. Dad introduced them as Big John, he was a doctor from Kansas City, along with George from the same place. Dad had hired Joe Dagg as an extra guide that was required when hunting. They unpacked their supplies down at the dock by our boathouse. Our canoes were left at English River. Dad had stored them on the shore, right side up, and sprinkled some bleach inside so that the animals would stay away. The bleach was in a large flat pan so that it gave off a good stench.

We had two boats with outboard motors. Joe Dagg was in charge of one boat and dad in the other. We packed all the supplies, guns, fishing equipment, clothing, food and staples. Dad did a quick check that we had enough gas that was properly mixed with oil. He stood at the dock like a captain giving the final operations orders, as everyone got into the boats. Joe Dagg was with the two Americans, then Dad and I with our supplies. Dad then spoke up saying we were going first to English River Falls where there were two canoes. He said we'd then portage our canoes and supplies to Lac Suel, the lake above the falls.

Jim Chief and Tootimah would meet us there to have our lunch. After that the plan was to paddle the canoes to the trapping cabin.

———————————————————————————————

Chapter Twenty-Three

We were on our way. The morning sun was dancing on the water ahead of us, as we skimmed across the mirror of the lake. As usual I admired the beauty and majesty of the landscape. It is always like a postcard of color that only nature could make for our pleasure and use, as we may need it. This includes all the wildlife and fish in the lakes. Imagine being given all of this totally and completely free as well as the clear clean water with the air we breathe. The relaxing atmosphere along with the purr of the motor put me to sleep because I opened my eyes just as dad slackened off on the throttle. The boat shrugged itself onto the sandy shore with a thud. Joe Dagg steered his boat next to ours in the same manner. We climbed out of the bow pulling the boats up for unloading.

Big John lumbered out of the boat while Joe and George steadied it. Both men stood and gazed across the lake slowly turning to the shoreline and the bush. Big John the M.D. commented on the fresh air. "You got that right," was George's reply.

Dad and Joe and I were busy unloading both boats, placing the goods on the shore. Dad took one boat motor off and placed it in the middle of the boat covering it with a small canvas and Joe did the same in his boat. We then pulled the boats up onto the shore onto the rocks. They each put a small filler can of gas up in the bow with the cap off.

I noticed they forgot the gas cap. Dad said the cap was left off because the animals smell that gas and it acts like a repellant.

Everyone had their packsacks on their backs along with four paddles which Joe and dad carried. We had about three-quarters of a mile to get to the top of the falls, which roared intensely as we approached closer. We had to walk alongside the falls to the top. Jim Chief's secret method came back to me as soon as we had arrived. My pack felt light as I walked without any effort. I moved past the others in anticipation of seeing Jim Chief and Tootimah. I had an inner feeling that they would be there waiting. I came over the knoll and there was Jim with his outstretched arms along with Tootimah and her black tooth smile. I gave each a small hug of acknowledgement.

We greeted the rest of them when they arrived. Dad introduced the two American hunters, saying they were there to hunt moose. "This man is Big John and back in America he is a medical doctor. The other man here is George who is specialist who knows all about rocks." Jim gave a nod in acknowledgment and accepted the introduction.

Jim motioned to dad. "I have your canoes over here out of the wind," he said. Tootimah boiled some pinesap she got from the trees and put some on the canoes so that the animals will not touch them. It works the same as gas except it lasts a long time. There they are Onni; your son can put them down by the lake. Jim looked at me and said, they are ready to move when you want and you can get us some fish because you all must be hungry. I see you have your fishing rod and minnow net. There are minnows in that rocky spot as he pointed to the spot and then said good fish straight out from there." I was on my way as the rest found a good spot to make a fire.

I got my equipment and down I went. Once again amazing there were minnows and I scooped some up, taking one out then threading it on the hook leaving the net sit in the water so that the others could not escape. The hook no sooner hit the water than I had a strike and reeled in a three pounder.

Big John and George came down with their rods, I threaded a minnow on each hook and they cast out into the lake. Reeled their lines in without a strike. It was my turn. I cast out to the spot Jim had suggested with a fresh minnow and there it was another strike as I hauled in another three-pounder. How do you do that George asked. I don't know I guess I am lucky. They fished while I caught two more and brought them up to the campsite, as Joe was ready to fillet them. They called up saying that there are no more minnows left. We have enough fish anyway dad shouted down. The two men walked back up shaking their heads in wonderment. Tootimah and Jim looked at me with a slight grin knowing how it works.

Dad and Joe were the self-designated cooks. They placed a devise made from iron rods that looked like two large flaps of a book with rods from each end which held a heavy screen tray. This was all placed over the fire. It made a perfect top for the iron frying pan plus the metal coffee and teapots.

The crackle of the fire with the odor of fish frying along with the distinct aroma of coffee after Joe dumped coffee into the boiling water. Joe had to immediately remove the coffeepot from the heat so it wouldn't boil over from the foam. Dad quipped to Joe, when are you going to learn how to make coffee. Remember you take the pot off first and the same for tea and let it sit. The coffee you let simmer.

Dad kept the fried fish in a large pan beside the fire. He had twelve fillets of pickerel (walleyes are what the Americans call them). He had large tin plates with knives and forks, ready with warm scones that mom had provided for the trip. No other frills, tin plates, tin cups and any place you could find to sit on the ground. Come and get dad announced.

It is amazing that when you are hungry you have no time to think about things like mashed potatoes, vegetables, gravy and condiments. Jim Chief and Tootimah joined in after everyone else had taken their portions after pouring their tea. Thank you Onni, Jim said as he went back and sat cross-legged on the ground.

It is a pleasure to have you both here with us sharing our food with you. I know this has great meaning to you Jim. These men from America have never shared a meal with people of your origin or way of life. They are what we call city folk. Big John over there as he pointed to him which he acknowledged with a short wave. Jim he is a man of medicine he is a healer of people. Maybe he could fix my teeth Jim said with a grin showing his black teeth. Then our next man is George who knows all about rock. Jim gave him a nod as he said rock is not hard to find here. We are going to go to my trapping shack today to stay while we are hunting. We will see you there before we go to hunt tomorrow, dad annouced." Yes", Jim answered.

Chapter Twenty Four

We sat in the solitude for awhile as I reflected around us and the thought came to me. We are sitting in the greatest cathedral in the world. A limitless ceiling with surroundings that is in constant change. That shows different colors four times a year and each change with insurmountable beauty. Jim was standing beside me and he put his hand on my shoulder when he said I glad to see you giving thanks for all of the beauty that has been given to us. Tootimah put her hand on my other shoulder. With both hands on me, gave me a surge of energy that had a great feeling of unity with love. It was a deep and effective experience.

The others had gone down to the canoes and were loading them up as Jim and Tootimah were making sure the fire was completely out. The dishes and the outdoor fire stove were packed. I had to give my head a shake because where had I been as I had not noticed anyone moving about getting ready to go. Jim looked at me and said, you need not worry because you were with the Great Spirit in your thoughts. You will get used to being with the Spirit. Let us get down to the shore, as they are ready to go.

You are right Jim I suppose I will have to get use to being with the Great Spirit and be able to recognize it. In other words Jim would other people even notice me when I am with the Great Spirit?

The other people will not notice your movements even though you are right there because you will be in harmony with the Great Spirit Jim answered.

We proceeded down to the landing where the canoes and everybody else was. They were almost ready to get going to dad's trapping cabin.

Dad came over to talk to Jim because he would get the weather for the next few days for their hunting. Jim said you should get to the small bay in the early morning because the runting time has started and you should be able to get a good bull to come down to the shore when you use my old bull-moose call.

"Yes I know what to do Jim. When we have some time after the hunt my tourist friends from the United States would like to have a talk with you. Would that be all right Jim?"

Jim looked up and said: "I guess so but what do I know because these men have gone through big schools in America?"

"Yes Jim," dad answered. "But they would like to talk to you about your way of life and how you understand and know the Great Spirit."

"I will come and talk to these men after the hunt because you have always been my best friend Onni. Your son knows all these things now as well as I do all he needs is more experience, which will be given to him. He will be guided as to how much he should say about his abilities but more by his actions that he does. It will be up to him."

Joe Dagg had to paddle the canoe with the two Americans. They were unable to help Joe because they had no experience of how to handle a canoe or paddle one. Joe just kept on paddling and chewing his tobacco with an occasional spit into the water that left a brown spot in the clear water. His chin was wet with juice of his chew. Joe was busy.

Dad and I were the last to leave, as we had to find out when Jim would come by to see us at the shack. I paddled at the front, as dad was experienced in paddling and steering at the same time. He knows how to use the paddle grip at the top to give it a turn at the right time.

The small trapper shack came into view just as the sun was speeding into the western sky. The shack was nestled under huge jackpine trees with a high cliff of rock twenty feet to the rear that was on the north side as the shack faced south east in order to get most of the sunlight and warmth. It was an ideal spot for protection from the elements. Jim had also told dad that the sun would warm the rock during the day and hold the warmth.

The shore at landing was a mixture of rock and gravel as I jumped out to bring the canoe up onto the shore. We were in a small inlet the size of an average living room. We were first to arrive. Dad had steel animal traps hanging on the tree branches in the area. I noticed a trap that had a steel punch with the letter O on it. That was for Onni. It was a cardinal sin for another trapper to take and use fellow trapper's traps. They all had a mark on them.

Everyone was busy getting the supplies out of the canoes as Joe; dad and myself carried the supplies, food, water and sleeping bags up to the shack. Dad opened the door of the shack going inside he turned and asked Joe to get some kindling so that he could start a fire in the stove. Joe brought some dry kindling as well as an armful of dry cedar boughs which when burned in the stove would deodorize the inside of all the stagnated air. The fire got started as a puff of smoke came out of the stovepipe on the roof. Dad came out and looked at the smoke when he said that smoke would let Jim Chief know we have arrived here safely.

The cabin was made of six-inch diameter logs, which were three-buck saw lengths or twelve feet long. These uniform size logs were used for walls roof and floor. Dad had brought in one inch by eight-inch pine boards that were ten feet long. He used these for the floor. There was a stove made from a gasoline barrel that cut in half with the bottom on four bricks and steel bars across to the bricks. The topside had a thin steel plate over the top you could use for heating water and cooking. The end had a small square door for firewood. The cabin got warm in a matter of moments. The smokestack was installed over the steel sheet. It had two double bunk beds and one single made out of wood. Dad said he dried the innards of some bears they had hunted and put them under the shack floor which would keep all the little varmints away plus weasels otter and minks. A small table by the window used when dad was there alone in the winter trapping.

Joe was outside getting the fire and the contraption for cooking ready. He already had the coffeepot on as well as all the pans. I immediately knew what my job was and that was to go and get some fresh fish for a hearty supper. I was on my way made my way down to the lake remembering what Jim Chief had taught me and I began to say his words for guidance my eyes moved directly to a small crevice by the lake. They're as though trapped were minnows that I picked out and put them on the shore placing one on my hook. The first cast brought me a nice three pounder as well as four other casts and I had enough. I was totally elated at my experience. I brought them up and Joe was waiting with his fillet knife to get them ready. Dad acknowledged as he said, when you know what to do it is very simple son. Yes, dad I answered.

I did my house work and dad announced the sleeping bags are all on the bunks so we could eat and decide on our plans for the morning. We had a hearty meal. I was ready to get into my bunk. I only took off my boots and pants as I jumped into the bunk. The pillow was my rolled up pants.

It was just sunrise when dad nudged me to get my towel and soap. We were on our way to the shoreline to have our wake up wash. The water was chilly. The rest of our party followed when we all got freshened up. No shaves any hairstyling except for combing that we all did and after that it was on caps or hat. Dad always wore an old homborg gray hat. We all took our trip into the bush to do private business. Joe had the coffeepot going where the wonderful odor permeated the fresh morning air. That was topped off with a package of bacon frying on the skillet. Joe had more than a dozen eggs that he had cracked into a large pot on top of the makeshift stove. This was his way of making scrambled eggs as he constantly stirred them with a wooden spoon. We were all lined up and ready for our breakfast. We had nice crusty buns that mom had put into the lunch box.

The buns had that taste that just never leaves your taste buds. It was years later that my brother and I found a small restaurant that made hamburger steak exactly like mother used to fry them. It is amazing how we know immediately. The taste buds never forget.

Dad broke the silence when he pointed out to the lake and said, let's make some strong Indian tea because Jim Chief will be coming around the point in a few minutes. I wondered how dad knew but all of a sudden there he was. His canoe slid up onto the shore as dad guided and held it until Jim stepped out when he gave dad a greeting.

I had a sense of excitement when Jim arrived. All of us were there to greet him when Jim announced that hunting today would not be that good because the full rutting season would not start until tomorrow. The rutting season is a time when male and female moose are attracted to each other for about three weeks or so.

Dad brought Jim up to the campfire and had him sit in dad's chair as Joe poured Jim a cup of tea the rest of us had some more coffee.

John G. Makie

After everyone got comfortable dad said, Jim, my tourist friends from the United States would like to talk about your way of life and how you know the Great Spirit that you have so gratefully passed on to my son.

Chapter Twenty Five

Jim turned saying, Onni you have the Great Spirit except for the gifts your son has because you have always been my best friend and you never let me down. What is it that these men want to know?

Big John was the first ask. Did you know we were here last evening?

Yes Jim said because I saw your smoke when Onni started the fire in the shack. My tent is on the other side of that hill as he pointed with his hand. Come I will show you as he stood up and started to walk to the side of the rock cliff behind the shack. He found a trail that we were not aware of and started the climb. I was behind Jim as he walked up the steep hill like a young man. The others lagged behind after we were already at the top. Jim found a log to sit on as the others slowly came up and joined him. Jim said, you are now going to see the land and water of the Great Spirit as his arm made an arc of what your eyes can see.

Joe Dagg was the last one to come up as he said you guys with your long legs, walk too fast. He had a big wad of snuff in his lip, which oozed from the side of his mouth in a slow drip.He, was not a poster boy.

Both of the tourists had their cameras out getting pictures of the beauty that they were looking at. They could see for miles as Jim came over and pointed towards his tent, as we had to focus very intently. Big John focused his zoom lens camera through which he could spot the campsite. Jim said that the camera behind our eyes has already recorded everything here and we can recall the picture anytime we want.

Dad came over and announced that we should now go back down, as we should not take up too much time of Jim. Joe came by and said," Onni this is harder than skinning a big moose going up and down this hill".

They all arrived back at the campsite a little tired from the climb. Dad made sure everyone was properly seated around so that Jim could answer any questions the tourists had to ask.

Chapter Twenty Six

Big John was the first to start the questions. Mr. Chief, as Jim interrupted saying, I am only Jim to all of you here. Big John asked, how did you know Onni had arrived here because you came over.

Onni and I have an understanding that he always makes a fire in his shack stove so when I see the smoke come out, I know. I noticed that you have those special glasses that you can see for miles around from up on the hill. From the hill we can see about eight miles but with your glasses you can see twice as far. If we can find a spot like this think of the animals because they live here all the time. Yes Jim nodded; they have lived here for a very long time. It is their house; they have many ways to know who comes into their house. They get fooled when some one comes from up wind or they make a mistake and a hunter finds them. Onni is a smart hunter because he knows how the moose thinks as well as other animals.

Onni smiled with a sense of gratefulness and said, it was Jim who taught him all the ways of the bush. Jim was born into this way of life and he is a part of it.

Jim held out his hand and said he would go to his tent because Tootimah would be expecting before the storm, which was coming soon. He looked at Onni saying this man knows where to find your prize animal. He is a good guide.

They watched as Jim walked into the bush as he would walk home. The sky begins to fill with large rolling clouds slowly picking up momentum. George looked up and said, this is an observation augury, like a prophetic sign. Onni he said I really feel safe with you because you are with us. Onni gave a tip of his hat in recognition. Large white caps were forming on the lake as they all moved towards the safety of the cabin.

How long will this storm last, George asked.

Onni looked over at him and said, do you hear any birds? No squirrels around either, there are not any movements of wild life. They have all found they're safe places and all on the ground in case of falling trees or branches from the wind. We will have three or four hours of heavy storm and then it will clear up. In the mean time let us go into the shack and I will bring in some dry wood for the stove so we can have a good cup of tea and talk or snooze, whatever you want. After tea I will start supper.

No sooner had they had some tea when the rain started to pour down driven by the wind with hard claps of thunder and lightening we could see from the shack window across the lake and then we could not even see the lake for solid rain. It seemed like it would go on indefinitely. We had a hard time hearing each other as the storm continued on. Dad had put a rain cover on the stovepipe so the fire kept on going.

The big pot of water was boiling and Dad put a handful of tea into a separate pot that had a spout on it and then poured in the hot water. He said that you have to let it sit for awhile so if you don't like it to strong you can have some now. Both Big John and George took their tin cups over and filled them three quarters full. The rest of us followed suit.

We sat on the bunks, as there was only one wooden chair which dad sat on. Joe Dagg and I sat on a bunk. It felt very comfortable as the dampness was taken away by the stove heat. The atmosphere was of camaraderie and fellowship.

Onni pulled out his snuffbox. Tapping the lid twice he opened it and with two fingers loaded it into his lower lip.

George immediately said, holy Christ Onni you mix that snuff with some of this tea it must be powerful to swallow.

Not at all Onni said, I don't let the tea touch the snuff as he gave a short laugh as he sat back in his chair when he asked, well fellows what did you think of today, at least up to now. We didn't go out for moose but you had a chance to meet with Jim.

I must admit, George started off. That Jim sure startled me when all of a sudden I saw this Indian standing there. I was struck by some kind of sense that he just appeared out of thin air. At the same time a sort of calmness pervaded my whole being. Strange I suppose but with wonderment and comfortableness which I can not explain.

Onni turned over to George saying, yes, that is the sort of way Jim Chief has been ever since I have known him. He has never told me how he can do those things. I like to think of him as my very best friend who seems to turn up at exactly the right time. Tootimah does not make herself seen very much but one time during a storm like this one I spent it in their tent. When she makes tea, she makes it from roots, plants and leaves from a Tamarack tree. Jim told me to drink it because it is very healthy. No one knows how old Jim is or Tootimah because they were here when I came in 1911. Hell, he was old then, who knows but he prances around a lot better than any of us, including my son here. He certainly has a wonderful gift and his abilities to do things that baffle me as to where he gets this strange power.

George broke the silence by saying; let us all turn in now and continue this in the morning. They all got into their sleeping bags after taking off pants and shirts. Zippering up the sides and adjusting their pillows each responded with good night.

Chapter Twenty Seven

The forest was coming to life as daylight started to show itself over the trees and the lake had a slight haze of fog over it. Onni was the first to make his way down to the lakeshore, with his soap and towel. He sat leaning up against the boat as he took off his long underwear that he flipped over the side of the boat. He picked up his soap as he slowly waded into the water and started to lather himself. George and Big John were on their way down as well with towels and soap. One said to Onni, holy molly you will freeze in that water. Not at all Onni replied it just makes you nice and fresh to start the day. You are not fooling Big John said as he eased himself into the water. This water is ready to form ice. George just stood by the boat after that statement and splashed water on his face while washing his hands. Onni and Big John came out of the lake drying themselves as they wrapped their towels around them.

They moved up to the shack in a hurry where I had the fire going and the stove was warm and the shack was warming up fast. We went outside and got the forty five-gallon drum that was cut in half. The drum had holes on the bottom for air. With the help of some gasoline the fire got going in a hurry. An iron bar rests on two prongs at each end. The water can was hung on this for morning coffee. What an aroma it produced when Onni threw in a handful of coffee.

The sun was now dancing on the water with flickers like diamonds sparkling. The rays of the sun displayed the evergreens as well a bringing out the full colour of the birch trees that had some of their bark curled up. You could smell the moss in the ground from the moist hue it had gathered in the night. Moss always grows on the south side of a tamarack tree it acts like a compass when you are in the bush. From the camp the lake now looked like a mirror. Not even a ripple on the water. The shoreline projected itself into the water. What majesty, peace and serenity this all gave us. Free upon our awakening.

The silence was broken with the placing of a paddle on the side of our boat at the lake. Jim Chief and Tootimah had arrived. Tootimah held the canoe steady while Jim climbed out. They pulled the canoe on to the shore. Jim pointed toward the shack as he started to lead the way.

Onni spoke to the two Americans in a wiser saying, listen to try and hear them walking up towards them. They could not hear a sound they were amazed. Their movements made no sound as they walked in their moccasins.

Onni lifted his hand gesturing, for Jim and Tootimah to sit down on the board benches that were perched on two tree stumps. Jim nodded and they both sat down. Welcome to our camp Onni said. I will boil you up some, tea as they both nodded. Onni got a can with a wire handle on it, filled in some water and placed it over the fire on the rod. He took the can off the fire as it boiled very quickly. He then reached into can with the tea and threw in a handful. There he said that is real Indian tea. By the way, I will need some Tamarack from the woodpile so that I can place the heavy frying pan on them. Tamarack will not burn, as fast so it is good to hold the pan, Onni added.

Big John had placed a pound of thick bacon in the large cast iron pan ready for frying. Placing it on the Tamarack wood it heated up in a few minutes and began to sputter giving off an aroma of country style breakfast. In another can the coffee can was simmering with fresh coffee in it. It gave off the aroma of coffee. Combined it could attract anyone on the lake. Next came the eggs that were dumped into the frying pan after the bacon was removed. One dozen.

Jim looked over at the cooking when he said, you could get used to eating in the bush if you stay here. It is a friendly place and the bush will like you if you like the bush. Jim then looked sideways, after hearing a crackling sound in the bush from behind the shack. A bear Jim said.

Onni got up slowly and went inside the shack. He got a rifle, pointed it up in the air and fired a shot. He put the rifle down beside his stump, sitting down he said, Now we can have breakfast.

One of the Americans asked, what do you mean Onni, that we can have breakfast now.

Jim Chief interrupted stating, the bear would stay away until they had all left the campsite. At this time of year bears look for all the food they can eat. We are not that far from his den where he will spend the winter. He will go to sleep so that he will not use up much fat.

He will be back Onni said, so we had better remember to leave all the canoes right side up today and during the night. Putting some birch brows into the canoe will help with keeping off the smell of any food that may have been there. I will hang up some honey in a can up in the tree tonight so that we can hear the bear when he comes around. He will go for the honey and make a grunting noise as soon as he smells it.

Jim and Tootimah were nodding approval while Onni was talking. Onni never knew if Tootimah understood or talked any English, he had only heard her talk to Jim in Indian.

Onni leaned over to Jim and whispered in his ear and they both went into the shack. When they both came out Onni had several pieces of round bread that was called hard tack. It is Scandinavian bread made without yeast so that as long as you keep it dry it will last for a long time. Here is your bread Jim, Onni said. Jim gave Onni a smile that turned his old wrinkles and face into a complete smile. Black teeth and all. His eyes sparkled which appeared out his wrinkled eyebrows. He was a picture of contentment.

Jim cracked a round piece in two and gave Tootimah one half, who gave a smile of appreciation to Jim and Onni. In her own individual way she looked radiant beside the fire stooped over as she looked up. They both dipped the bread into the bacon grease to soften up good, as they had to use their gums to chew.

Onni offered the bacon and eggs to all of us. We all tried the same thing that tasted good out there in the bush. Onni put his bacon on top of the hard tack. Shortly the flies and bugs were starting to congregate to get their share. We started to clear up the breakfast plates and utensils. Breakfast was over.

After the meal everyone went down to the dock. We gathered all the gear we would need for the day. Jim Chief and Tootimah put their canoe in the water and carefully pulled it up alongside the dock. George and Big John carefully put their rifles into the canoe, one each to where they were going to sit.

Jim saw that George had a scope on his rifle. He said, I guess you can shoot a long distance with that kind of a sight?

Several hundred yards with good accuracy, George responded.

What does he mean Onni? asked Jim.

He can hit an animal on that shore way over there, Onii said, pointing to a shoreline about three hundred or more yards away. He can hit an animal and have a clean kill.

Jim nodded with a slight smile saying you would have good eyes without that sight to shoot that far. I always get close with my 30-30 rifle. We only shoot when we need meat and only in the fall time. I mostly use snares and traps. Shells cost money and they scare the animals then they can get wet and they are no good.

Chapter Twenty Eight

They all stood and gazed at nature's beauty of forest and water particularly as they looked to the distant bay where the shoreline reflected into the mirror like calm water. You could see the perfect picture of the trees only they were upside down. There was a thin layer of misty like fog that had tubes of sunlight shining through and touching the water that seemed to go into the depts. In an unseen part of the lake came the sound of a wild duck. Jim said the duck is across the lake swimming on the shore among some fallen trees. It all felt like a force of creative goodness that gave a feeling of well being. Jim turned to Onni and said, we know eh! Onni, we know.

Yes Jim we know, Onni answered.

Jim turned and shook the hand of all three men and then gave Onni an Indian hug with one arm on the back then he stepped into his canoe. Tootimah held the canoe study and each took up their paddles. Jim turned to George and Big John saying, both of you will find this Great Spirit. Then with a parting gesture with his hand he said and waved. This great space and land you will always remember.

On a final word he said to Onni I will tell you where to hunt today, when we get out to the middle of the lake. O.K. Onni? His canoe was on its way with only a slight ripple as they both paddled.

O.K. Jim, I will wait for your words, Onni said.

Chapter Twenty Nine

George immediately asked Onni, inquisitively. What does he mean he will tell you from the middle of the lake because that is almost a mile away.

Onni turned to him. You just watch and listen when Jim gets to the middle of the lake. By this time they could not distinguish Tootimah from Jim only the harmony of their paddles. Then their movement of the paddles suddenly stopped. Jim's voice came to them as though they were standing right beside them. He said, I am pointing my paddle to the Eastern Shore and right there at the mouth of the river in the bay, in late afternoon you will have two moose. Then in harmony again they kept paddling and all of a sudden they were out of sight.

I know the place very well so we can start to get things arranged because we will have made our kill of a prize trophy for each of you. It is cold enough so that we can transport them back with us. You can then strap them onto your cars for the trip back home, Onni stated.

Big John was still standing in disbelief as he said Jim sounded like he was next to us speaking, absolutely amazing.

He was about two miles away, Onni said, but the water is calm as he motioned to the high shoreline as well as the trees. His voice carries from certain places and by the way did you see their canoe after they started paddling.

No they both answered almost together. He just disappeared. How did he disappear like that, George wondered?

I have noticed him do that many times, Onni answered. I asked him once about that. He said that he gets this certain energy inside himself and no one can notice him. That is why he can show up in odd places when you least expect him especially when you are in the same part of the country that he is in. He said that I must have been thinking about him. When you picture a person in your thoughts and it is received by his inner energy. This gives him the direction and he is transported there. I could not figure that out but it seems O.K. when you see him. I don't even get excited anymore.

Big john answered by saying, I have heard the fact that where the thought goes there the energy flows. That must be what happens in his case.

Maybe Onni quipped.

With hand on his chin, brushing his whiskers, George said you know that many centuries ago there was a man from Galilee that asked for a boat to talk to the multitudes that were on the shore. The boat moved out onto the water. No one knows exactly how far and He used the same principal. They could all hear Him very well as he delivered His sermon.

Let us get into the canoe and go out about the spot where Jim and Tootimah were. Onni suggested. They got into the canoe carefully. George in the center and Big John up front with his paddle then Onni in the rear to guide the canoe. They shoved off and moved at a rapid pace. Big John interrupted the paddling saying we should stop because I feel as though we entering a space where there is a surge of a wonderful feeling going in and through me a feeling of comfortableness and joy. Unexplainable with a complete freedom of self.

You are right John, George answered. There is this feeling as you say. This is the spiritual force Jim was telling us about. I feel very strong in this spot right now. This joy my friends is the joy of a spiritual experience and it feels like we all have it and will remember this feeling and cherish it for the rest of my life.

So will I Big John responded.

Now you know why I have trapped this area for so long. I told my friends and other people but they just said Onni you have been talking too much with old Jim Chief. I offered but no one wanted to come out and experience this like you fellows have. There is power here, he concluded.

They started paddling back to the dock with a look of serenity on their faces. They gazed at the beauty that surrounded them.

As they paddled quietly George broke the silence. You fellows know that I feel as if I have come through a metamorphosis the cocoon that I have lived in has opened up and I can see things differently. I don't know how but I do.

They nudged the canoe up to the dock in complete silence. They were all joyous in their own contentment. They were happy joyous and free.

Chapter Thirty

Onni tied up the canoe as they left all of their gear in the canoe ready for the afternoon hunt. They all moved in a happy mood as they completed their individual personal duties. The feeling of their experience was with them as they could meditate feelings in response to their innermost selves with humility to the creative intelligence of the universe.

Later Onni and George went up into the shack for a short snooze while Big John was so overwhelmed that he just went for a walk in the bush.

Upon their awakening and John's return they made themselves a good trappers lunch of balogna, garlic sausage and bread. They used water for a chaser. They ate heartily as they needed the energy for the hunt.

Let's go boys, Onni announced, it would be time when we get there. You will experience another one of Jim's promises as it comes true. Onni checked his knife, axe, and rope with a pulley and a large funnel. Once all set in the canoe with rifles by their sides, they began to paddle towards the Eastern Shore line. They all took a short glance to the center of the lake where they had that experience as they paddled in anticipation of the hunt. The sweet scented odor of pine drifted as the glided over lily pads with flowers of white popping up from the depths below. The sun looked like it was getting ready to take its last look around. Soon it would start to change its color into a crimson haze before departing for the day in the western sky.

This exciting experience Onni almost whispered, will be with you as long as you live. You will take it with you in your memory bank. It will be like your mother's favorite cooking with one taste you will know. Remember a thought travels over distance and space because if we can bring our thought over thousands of miles then think of how this was given to us by The Great Power. He travels by thought and feeling.

The canoe nudged it's nose around the point of land to the bay where our hunt was to take place. They were moving closer to the spot where Jim Chief had pointed.

There in the picture postcard setting up to her knees was a beautiful specimen of a cow moose with her head feeding in the calm water. Everyone was hardly breathing when Onni slowly took the large funnel and put it in the water without any noise. He slowly puled it out which was filled with water holding his finger on the spout. He then lifted it up over his head and holding over the water let go and the water spilled out onto the lake. It made a sound comparable to a cow moose urinating. The cow moose immediately raised its head to look around.

Onni put his finger to his lips for everyone to keep quite. He knew that the cow moose could not see them as the sun set protected them. The moose continued to feed. The silence was broken with the sound of another moose coming through the bush down to the shore. The big Bull Moose broke out into the open. He was a magnificent specimen, as he stood wide-eyed gazing at the cow moose that looked up at him.

Onni motioned his arms to quiet the men but pointed to their rifles. It had been agreed that each one would take a shot at the big bull. They could then share the hunt and the kill. They had their back to the setting sun so vision was perfect as the bull moved gracefully towards the cow in the water. Their rifles were pointed and at the ready as Onni nodded and they both fired. The big bull was hit and moved to shore where he fell. The cow took off as fast as she could run. The hunt was over.

Big John and George were still shaking after the exciting experience as Onni paddled to the shore. He said that head of the Bull Moose was facing the sun so he would not see us anyway if he were still alive. The bullets had hit their mark and they had a clean kill.

Onni said, you have to have a big wall to mount this rack in your club house and it will hang there for a very long time. Congratulations! Now you can take your pictures before I bleed him. Both of you can stand by the rack in the water while I take the picture for you. Maybe a couple so we make sure. They got the camera ready while Onni snapped the pictures. They then took each other's as well as one of Onni.

The prize trophy animal came down the slope to the waters edge when Onni taunted him with his funnel filled with water. The sound effects sure brought him down like a thundering bull huge and magnificent.

Now the hard work had to start as Onni went to canoe and fetched the rope and pulley to move the moose into a good position to bleed him which was a necessity as soon as possible. Onni got the winch system set up to maneuver his huge head closer to the water. He dug a small trench beside his head so that all the blood would go into the lake. The two hunters were unable to watch Onni as he took out his big hunting knife to cut in exactly the right place. He did and there was a gush. The water turned red and slowly filtered out into the bay. Onni cut a small birch tree down the cut a pole sharpening both ends so they would pierce through the leg muscles by the hoof. He moved the rope to the pole and attached the pulley, calling the men to help. Boys he said, this is a twelve hundred pound animal so we need muscle. They got the chore done. Now I will cut him open while we wait for my son to come from camp. He will bring the saw, big axe and some old clothing I brought to put over on top and around the animal. That way the scavengers will leave it alone for the night besides I will make a little trench. Animals will not trespass over the trench because the clothing is a human smell. Those empty shells in the canoe we will leave on the moose.

No sooner had he finished that his son came around the point, with the boat and motor.

No one told him to come.

Onni just said, he heard two shots. That was his signal to come over to where we were hunting. Jim Chief probably heard the shots as well. He will be in to see us in the morning.

Onni and his son finished the trench around the great moose plus the clothing and spent shells on top. This would keep the scavengers away for the night until the smell wares off. Then in a few days the only thing left would be the massive bone skeleton. That is nature doing her work.

They all got into the big outboard boat with the canoe in tow. The two hunters and Onni could enjoy the trip back to the shack. The reflection in the water of the shoreline started to show a tint of crimson as the late sun was moving further into the western sky. You could even see the shadow of the boat along the shore.

George had a smile of serenity when he said, this then is the Universal Mind or Spirit of Nature all working in harmony even when man interferes to get his food freely and in great abundance. However, from this time forward I shall only hunt with my camera for trophies such as we have been given today.

The boat slowed with the engine shut off as it coasted to the dock while Onni at the front held his arm out for a cushion not to hit. They all got out of the boat with contentment on their faces. They were back home for the night to enjoy a good meal and fellowship.

Everyone did their personal chores as well as getting the open fire made in the fire pit where the damp embers had to be cleared out. The area was ready to start the cooking as Onni brought out the cooler that had the fish that was already filleted. Half a pound of butter into the big iron pan that sputtered as the fillets were placed in. The aroma of the cooking permeated the campsite. George opened up a large can of pork and beans that we could pass around.

Relaxation was the order of the evening to be spent near the fire as it was cooling off with a nice hot cup of coffee.

Onni broke the silence, while leaning with one elbow on a log for support; today was a real hand on experience. Not one you can learn from books but real genuine feeling. It reaches your innermost self. These experiences can change a person's path of life. It is like a prospector when he finds gold and looks down to see the mother load. The only way to keep it, we must share it.

I am convinced George started saying that nothing happens by mistake in this world of ours. Every instant, particularly in the last few days this has become so noticeable. My eyes and mind have been opened up to see, without a doubt, the Creative Intelligence of the Universe at work.

Big John responded, well stated George. I know I have searched for peace of mind in many different places. Sometimes from a bottle of whiskey sitting on a bar room stool asking the advice of a bartender because he was the only person that seemed to listen. Some times from the lure of soft music where companionship seemed paramount. Then the ultimate, going on hunting trip with my best friends. Thank God at least I have done the latter. Regardless of what I have done this powerful force of love and tolerance has been with me. Only now has the adjustment been made to focus on the Creative Intelligence. I shall never forget Jim Chief and Tootimah as long as I live.

The night sky was starting to darken. Joe and Onni went into the shack to light up the kerosene lamps as well as getting s fire going to take off the chill. It was about forty degrees outside as the fresh air of fall was coming. Everyone got in and snuggled into their sleeping bags. Sleep came quickly from the tiring day.

Onni and Joe were up at the break of dawn. They got the fire going with the coffee on. Joe was loading up what he needed to complete skinning and butchering the moose. He poured some coffee into a thermos along with hard tack and left overs he had put aside. He talked to Onni for a moment and he was on his way.

They had just poured their coffee along with a plate of breakfast when they heard a noise at the dock. There was Jim Chief with a wave as he came up the small embankment.

I was by where you shot the moose and believe he was the biggest in the bush. That is good because he will not be anymore good after this season anyway. You boys gave him a good retirement, Jim said. By the way the cow moose will have his kin. He then joined them having a coffee which he said was a treat because he just has tea at home. We can put the head of the moose in the center of the big canoe. It will be better to tow it to the landing so the train can pick it up. Joe knows how to prepare and do all that. We will cut up the rest. Are you boys going to take some home?

No Onni said because it is a lot trouble to take moose meat across the border and besides they have to make out papers for the head. If you fellows want the taxidermist in town do it and he will have it shipped to your place back home.

I think we will do that so that it can go directly to our lodge meeting place, George answered.

Jim was already out in his canoe as got into the boat with all the gear as Onni's son made the canoe ready with a tow rope so he didn't have to paddle alone. The morning was calm as they glided along looking back at the shack that had been home for the last few days. The hunters were taking pictures of all as well as Jim paddling up ahead as we were catching up to him. We turned the point and saw Joe busy doing the butchering. The sky had ravens and crows ready to clean up even dipping down to get a bite. Joe had the meat covered.

Chapter Thirty One

Joe pulled Jim's canoe up so that he could load it with meat for his winter needs. Jim said good man Joe. There will be enough for everyone. He motioned to Onni to go and sit on a log on the shore away from the rest. They went and sat down facing each other.

Onni I will not see you until next spring when I come in with Tootimah for the last time. She will be gone to her resting-place next fall. We are both prepared as she will go first then I will follow her in the summer or fall. I will be moved by the Spirit to go. She had a great dream telling her what to do. I will have the same dream when the time comes. Tootimah has made you a Deer hide Jacket with beads. She has put two colors on it to show how old she is and the other color to show how many years that she was married to me. I will leave it in your shack. Then after you have had it until you go to your rest, you can pass it on to your son. They both stood up and shook hands looking deep into each other's eyes and with a final jerk of handshake departed.

Jim paddles slowly away, not looking back. His Eagle feather in his hat stood straight up like an Ariel post. His motion was steady as the canoe moved straight which had a good load of winter meat. He would not have to hunt this winter except for fish, rabbits and partridge.

Tootimah was back at their camp getting ready for winter when Jim would trap for some furs to sell in the spring so that they could buy their needs for next year. She was old. Very old. She had gentleness about her that you could accept automatically. She and Jim had a noticeable bond they spoke only a few words, as they intuitively knew each other's thoughts. This was the Spiritual cord that bound them together. When they got married or how old they were. They didn't have a birth certificate. Jim was not yet noticeably as frail as Tootimah. He had deep reddish brown wrinkles even in the folds of his skin. Like aged tree bark. If he stood beside a tree he would blend right in. You could walk right by him without noticing in the bush. Although his face was aged his deep brown eyes had a twinkle of friendliness and compassion. Standing in his presence there was a sense spiritual well being and camaraderie.

It took the four men to place the moose head into the center of the canoe. Joe had covered the meaty area with habicure. This was a form of salt to keep it from starting to decay before it got to the Taxidermist in town. They would transport meat skin and all to the railway landing up at the far end of the lake. Joe would stay with it until the late afternoon train came by. They would stop when the flag was raised on pole arm by the track. Joe would leave the canoe under the landing. We went back to the shack and left the canoe on the canoe rack where it would not be disturbed

Onni said let us get going home because it is still calm and we have a good load so we can not go full speed. They were on their way.

Big John at the door of the shack

George with rifle and Joe Dogg.

About the Author

He was born and raised in a Hamlet in Northern Ontario Canada. He had his schooling in a small Railroad Centre close to the Hamlet. He is the son of Scandinavian parents who immigrated to

Canada in the early 1900's. He learned his basic English at the start of school where many others had immigrant parents that were unable to speak English. He only spoke Finnish at the time. His dad was a sawmill worker, fur trapper and guide for tourists that wanted to hunt for moose, deer or bear.

With a grade twelve education at the age of eighteen he joined the Canadian Naval Voluteer Reserve. He was a member of a commando force specializing in underwater demolition. He was a part of the SAT. Special Assignment Team. Due to his Oath of the Secrets Act of Canada he was not allowed to discuss his exploits for a period of fifty years after discharge. After this time he was awarded a pension for Post Traumatic Stress Disorder.

Upon discharge he took advatage of some veternan's schooling where he worked in various carreers prior to his retirement.

This book will take you on a journey where you can individually take your mind through boyhood fantasies. Exploring the impossible means of defying gravity by that of an outside power source. This old Indian and his wife could move silently in their moccasins and never disturb the land, always leaving it in it's original state. They were guided and cared for by this outside source. They intuitively knew the weather, the movement of animals, like built in guidance systems. They were not physically strong but lived in a constant spiritual harmony with the universe. They could paddle long distances and Jim Chief had the secret ability, through his contact with his Indian Spirit he could lift a very heavy canoe over land.

The time is in the nineteen thirtees when the outside world suffered a depression. Modern technology was not yet invented. They lived off the land using their learned abilities to survive in all seasons. They lived in constant commune with forest and animals. They all knew their place and also how the animals lived.

Jim Chief claimed this Spiritual Technology was given to him as a young boy. He told Onni that he wished to pass these gifts on to his youngest son. This was a high-lite in the young son's life which thrilled him with excitement.

It will create excitement even of the history of how super heavy stones were moved long distances in the building of pyramids, and light houses in Egyptian ports. Then to the great edifices of South America in Inca times. How did they realy move those multi ton pieces of granite stone. Did they have an art or did the method of communication become lost to time. This is the fire of imagination the book will ignite. There are unexplainable things that happened thousands of years ago. Why could Jim Chief not have these powers.

The mocassins were made by Tootimah his wife from Deer hide.

This raw hide was chewed by a squaw because the saliva slowly went into the hide to make it very soft and plyable. It was all made from one piece of hide. Even the thread was deer hide.

The American tourists in the book are true as Onni was a real guide that took hunters out to hunt. These men did meet Jim Chief where they learned the secret of talking accross still water. They did get a trophy animal. Joe Dagg was a real helper for Onni then the son who is the author.

ISBN 1-4140-5372-X
90000

9 781414 053721